ℬ Hannah's Voyage ☙

D1054340

Written by Josephine Croser
Illustrated by Steven Woolman

ETA
Cuisenaire

Hannah's Voyage
ISBN 0-7406-1023-6
ETA 352061

Revised American edition published in 2004 by ETA/Cuisenaire®
under license from Era Publications. All rights reserved.

ETA/Cuisenaire Product Development Manager: Mary Watanabe
Lead Editor: Betty Hey
Editorial Team: Kevin Anderson, Kim O'Brien, Nancy Sheldon,
  Elizabeth Sycamore
Educational Consultant: Geraldine Haggard, Ed.D.

ETA/Cuisenaire • Vernon Hills, IL 60061-1862
800-445-5985 • www.etacuisenaire.com

Printed in China.

04 05 06 07 08 09 10 11 12 13   10 9 8 7 6 5 4 3 2 1

Table of Contents

"Stop the wagon," the guard says,
"and get that man down."
"He's sick."
"He must work."
"He'll die."
"Stop the wagon."
The men stop heaving at the shafts.
The stone-laden wagon stands still
as two men lift their fellow convict
down from his stony bed.
"We're sorry," they say to him, ashamed.
The sick man does not shoulder the shaft,
but lies sweating and limp on the ground.
"Move the wagon!" shouts the guard.
"If he wants his supper, he'll walk."

4

Chapter 1
Fire

"Fire!"

The word echoed around the market square.

"Fire! The church is on fire!"

From coffeehouses, taverns, lodging rooms, and houses, people ran out to stare. Among the onlookers was a slender girl of about fifteen. She wore shabby shoes and a ragged, brown dress that was stained, yet smelled of fresh lavender. Her once-golden hair was knotted in a bunch of dark tangles. Hansy.

The crowd jostled as the fire wagons raced through.

"Is it a French plot?" asked an onlooker.

"Has Napoleon landed?" asked another.

"There's nothing to worry about," reassured a third.

Men with hoses, ladders, and buckets ran from the wagons. Hansy, caught in the surging crowd, fought her way free, pausing at last by the corner of the market square between the church and the Great Piazza. Flames erupted from the roof of the church and smoke billowed toward her.

A carriage approached, and Hansy saw fear in the eyes of the horses. A crash sounded from the church. Timbers fell. Sparks and flames soared higher, and the crowd drew back and gasped.

"Toby!"

A voice screamed from the crowd as a small boy darted forward. The horses pulled and reared as the boy ran near, and Hansy, seeing the danger, dived in and hauled him clear.

The boy was safe, but there beside the horses' hooves lay Hansy, still and bleeding.

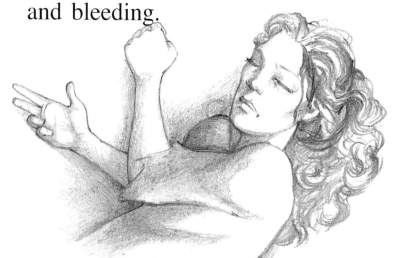

Chapter 2
The Family

The family carried Hansy into their room at the hotel. Outside, the fire continued to burn, but they no longer took notice.

"Don't look," said Mrs. Marsden, shielding her children from the sight of Hansy's injured head.

"It's her!" cried Louise. "John, you remember. The girl who saved me from that horrible, old woman."

"That was years ago," said Mr. Marsden, lifting Toby from John's arms.

"I'd know her anywhere," insisted Louise. "She said her name was Hansy."

The next morning, the market square at Covent Garden was especially crowded. In addition to the usual buyers and sellers, other people had come to stare at the ruined church.

Hansy had still not stirred.

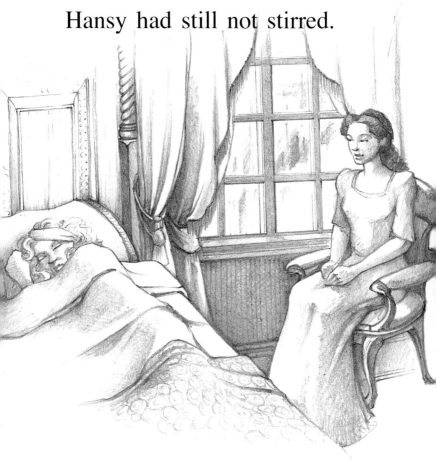

"I wish she'd wake up," cried Louise.

"The doctor said it would take time."

"Just because you're going to be a doctor ... oh, John, don't you wish you were coming with us?"

"Yes and no. Imagine the excitement of joining you later. The new colony is bound to need doctors."

Toby ran into the room. Louise hugged him, then stroked Hansy's hand.

"See the scar there?" she murmured. "I noticed it when I gave her my basket all those years ago. I wonder if anyone's missing her — or if anyone in the market can tell us about her."

Chapter 3
Questions

John and Louise entered the rowdy market to look for someone who might know Hansy.

"Her dress smells of lavender," said Louise. "Why don't we split up and try the flower stalls first?"

Louise hurried from stall to stall. It was autumn — pansies and asters abounded. Elsewhere in London, street vendors shouted out their wares, calling customers over to them, but at Covent Garden this was not the way. Louise had to walk around and look for lavender. As she walked, she found herself thinking about how different it might be in the new colony. Would the flowers be the same?

No one seemed to know Hansy. Or if they did, they weren't saying. At last a cheery woman pointed to a pair of twins.

"Ask them two," she said, nodding.

The twins looked to be about twelve. They stared suspiciously at Louise and refused to answer her questions until she bought flowers.

"Who wants to know?" asked one at last.

"She didn't come in last night," said the other. "We had to git all the water ourselves."

"Is she your sister?"

"Not likely. She's just a stray what our Ma took in. We've given her keep for years, then she stays out like this. Same thing happened years ago. Ma broke her leg when all us kids wus small. We had to go and find her — dressed like a boy and sleeping in the horses' straw, was our Hansy. But she come home when Molly begged her."

John had noticed Louise and joined her.

"Can you tell us her name and where she's from?" he asked.

"Can't tell ya nothing," said one twin.

"And wouldn't if we could," said the other.

Louise and John left reluctantly when the twins went quiet.

"Maybe they'd tell us more if we paid them," suggested Louise. But there was no need. Louise felt a tug on her dress. A small girl who was lame stared up at her.

"I can tell ya about Hansy," she said. "But tell her, if ya see her, Molly wants her back home."

Chapter 4
Answers

"Her real name is Hannah Brand," said Louise at lunch. "She came here years ago with her father. They brought vegetables to sell in the market, but he was arrested for someone else's crime and died in prison. She has no other family."

John took up the story they had learned scrap by scrap from Molly. "She stayed near the market waiting and waiting for her father. Then after he died, she had nowhere else to go, so she stayed here. She lives with a Mrs. Carver. There used to be someone called Lil, but Molly wouldn't say much about her. Just that she was very old and had died.

Hansy — Hannah — used to feed Lil and take care of her after her grandchildren ran off and left her alone. Molly thought one was arrested for stealing and the others disappeared soon afterward. Lately Hannah's been selling flowers from Lil's spot in the market.

"Any idea where Hannah came from?" asked Mr. Marsden.

"Molly said she often told her stories when the others were asleep. About fields with vegetables. There was a hill, and a heath. And when they drove into Covent Garden, she saw cows along the way. And St. Paul's — not the one that burned down, the big one with the dome."

Mr. Marsden frowned.

"Hampstead Heath," he mused.

"Highgate, perhaps. And Holloway Road. It would be worth a day of making inquiries. Our time is running out, but I'd like to tie up loose ends before we go. After all, we have her to thank for Toby being alive and well. Do you two want to come along?"

"Yes, sir," replied John.

"I'll stay here," said Louise, "in case she wakes up."

Chapter 5
Hansy Awakens

Hansy opened her eyes and saw a face. It blurred, then disappeared. She knew the face, from some time, some place. But when she tried to remember, her thoughts drifted off into darkness.

At other times, she heard voices and felt a gentle touch on her cheek.

Hansy had not really known her mother, who had died when she was young.

Now, floating on a strange softness, she touched the edge of her infant memories.

Each time she emerged, she felt peace, not alarm, and she sensed she was near Pa.

Next morning, Hansy awoke fully.

Beside her was a girl. Hansy was reminded of someone she'd met years ago — the girl she'd called the "rich girl." Could it really be her?

Louise saw her open eyes and smiled. Louise didn't talk, but simply held her hand.

"You saved our Toby," she whispered at last. "You were so brave!"

Hansy tried to remember.

"My name's Louise," she continued "and we've known each other for years, haven't we? You'll know my brother John when you see him, although he's all grown up, of course. Mother's been taking care of you, and Father …"

Louise stopped herself. It was too soon to talk about what Father had done.

It was also too much for Hansy. She looked at the bed. It was worlds away from the lice-ridden mattress she shared with Molly.

"Where am I?" she asked weakly.

"In the hotel where we stay sometimes. Near the Great Piazza." Louise hesitated, then squeezed Hansy's hand. "We have so much to tell you, Hansy. Hurry and get well!"

Chapter 6
Mr. Marsden Speaks

"It was a blacksmith," said Mr. Marsden. A few days had passed, and Hansy was now well enough to join them at the table. Never before had she seen such an array of china and cutlery. Nor so much food on a plate.

"I realized, Hannah, that since your father had a horse, he must have visited a blacksmith at some time. And I found one who remembered him."

Hansy's head spun. It was her first contact with that other life in many years.

When Mr. Marsden called her *Hannah*, it was as though he were speaking to another person, not her. Not Hansy, the girl who was always dirty, always hungry, always watching out for ways of staying alive, with gangs like Zia's ready to pounce and steal her earnings.

Hansy, the market girl … or Hannah, the country girl … who was she?

Mr. Marsden kept talking. The blacksmith had told him where Hannah's cottage stood.

"In time, it could be sold," said Mr. Marsden. "Someone's moved in, it seems, and the neighbors are using the fields."

"Can you tell her the rest, Papa?" asked Louise.

Both parents and even John shot her a quick look. "I mean, I just mean ..." she trailed off.

"Hannah," said Mr. Marsden seriously. "How important is it for you to remain with Mrs. Carver?"

Hansy dropped her fork.

Did she finally have a choice? Up till now, she'd *had* to stay there to survive. Joining Zia's band of thieves or being a "stable boy" were never good ideas.

"Molly's sweet," she began, "but Mrs. Carver and the twins …"

"… are something else!" announced John, and everyone laughed.

"Well, now that we've all agreed on that," continued Mr. Marsden, "we want to make a suggestion. Soon we'll be leaving England. Not John. He's staying here for his studies. But, the rest of us are sailing to Australia."

Hansy blinked. She'd never heard of such a place.

"It's on the other side of the world. We might not ever return to England."

Louise rushed in. "Uncle James is a minister in Australia, and he wrote to tell us that people who settle there are given land. You see, now that Grandfather's remarried, we're not rich anymore, or at least we can't keep our land and ..."

"Enough, Louise," interrupted Mrs. Marsden. "Let your father tell it."

"No," said Mr. Marsden. "She can take over from here."

"As long as she remembers," said her mother firmly.

"I'll remember," said Louise. Then she turned to Hansy, who by this time was feeling utterly lost.

"Hansy," she said. "We would like you to come with us. To Australia."

My leave papers.
A free man at last.
Penniless.
A criminal still,
in the eyes of the world.
But, my sentence cut short
and a parcel of land given to me
that I might coax crops
from the earth.
I must earn money for a ticket home
and find my girl.

Chapter 7
Louise Doubts

"Louise," said Hansy. "Do you know what happened to my dress?"

Mrs. Marsden had washed it, then put it aside.

"I'll find it," said Louise.

Hansy smoothed the skirt of the new dress she was wearing and thought of the two others packed for the voyage.

"I'd like to take it to Molly," said Hansy. And say goodbye, she thought.

"We can go together," said Louise excitedly.

Hansy stroked the back of one hand. The scar had faded over the years, but her habit remained.

"Market people can be difficult around strangers," she said. She wanted to go alone to say some private goodbyes, but didn't want to hurt Louise's feelings.

"They have a hundred places to hide, if they want to," she added.

Louise stared at Hansy. What if Hansy didn't want to come with them? What if she disappeared into the market and never came back? If that happened, Hansy might never learn the secret Father had discovered.

"Hansy," she began, handing her the dress. She held back, hoping her doubts didn't show. "You know something? I never know whether to call you Hansy or Hannah."

Hansy's eyes went between the stained, old dress in her arms and her new friend.

"I'll think about it," she said, "and tell you when I get back."

Chapter 8
Hansy's Goodbyes

Hansy felt strange as she ventured into the market square. It was her first time back since the night of the fire. Although the sounds and smells were familiar, her new dress made her feel like a stranger. She no longer belonged to the market.

Her first goodbye was to Lil. Sadly, she didn't know where Lil was buried — or Meg, for that matter. Probably in that scary corner beyond Drury Lane, where her fear of the rats and the suspicious people in rags prevented her from venturing.

She said goodbye to Lil in her heart as she sniffed the perfume from the flower stalls, remembering the old woman's smile.

Then leaving the market, she walked down toward the river and into Maiden Lane. When she came to a barbershop, she paused. There was the doorway she'd slept in one night when she'd been so desperate, and, beside it, the window where a boy's paintings had been displayed. Hansy felt the pocket of her new dress to touch the painting she had kept and treasured since that day.

And, in her heart once more, she said goodbye to the boy, William. Like John, he would be a young man now.

I hope you're still painting, she thought.

Winding her way back to the market, Hansy said goodbye to Meg. Meg had also lived on the streets, stealing whatever she could. It was Meg who had caused Pa's arrest, Meg who had told her that he had died in prison. Hansy had every reason to hate Meg, but she didn't. Meg had always watched out for her, and once more Hansy said goodbye to someone who was dead.

Zia and her band of little thieves — they would get no goodbye. At the thought of them, Hansy looked behind her, then hastened her step. Soon she was back in the market.

There were two more goodbyes to say.

The first, for which she wanted to be alone, was to Pa. She found the place where they'd stopped that first morning — Pa, herself, and their horse Bess. Hansy stood quietly for a moment. Someone bumped her with a basket, and a child knocked into her. Hansy stood her ground and tried to remember Pa's face. The shape of his face wouldn't come to her, but the memory of his kindness brought her warmth.

"Bye, Pa," she whispered. And in a flash, she knew what she wanted Louise to call her. Long ago, she had come to the market as Hannah. *Hansy* had been her street name, the name Meg had dubbed her.

She would leave with the name Pa had given her. *Hannah.*

Molly found Hannah before she had time to look for her.

"Tell your ma and the twins goodbye," she said, hugging Molly. "And be brave, little Moll. Don't forget you got pluck. And remember what else I taught you, eh? Never peel onions in bed!"

With that, Hannah thrust the dress into the child's bony hands, then hurried between the stalls toward the hotel. A sense of sadness overwhelmed her as she left the market, but then she looked up and saw Louise smiling as she approached. She knew that Pa would be happy for her, going away with this kind family.

Chapter 9
At Sea

Hannah lay in her bunk and listened to the sounds. The constant creaking of the ship was loudest, and beyond it, she heard waves and voices. Just now they were passing through windless hot air, and the children aboard were fretful.

The early risers were clattering their breakfast utensils, the late ones coughing or snoring. There was almost no privacy between decks. Hannah knew all the habits and moods of the other passengers, for they had been crammed together for several weeks now.

"Hungry?" asked Louise.

"As long as it's not green biscuits,

full of worms," said Hannah. One of the sailors had talked to Mr. White, who'd talked to Mr. Lane … tales made the rounds quickly. The time on board had increased Hannah's knowledge considerably.

"That's what the convicts had," Louise recalled, then suddenly clapped a hand over her mouth. Hannah knew that this ship was carrying passengers and goods, not convicts. Louise's reaction seemed rather strange. Hannah loved Louise dearly, but sometimes she felt puzzled when Louise started to say something, then suddenly stopped.

"How's Toby?" Hannah asked, to change the subject.

"Asleep at last. So's Mama."

Maybe today the family would

go up on deck to look around. Sometimes they saw birds or fish, and once there was great excitement when they saw whales. Hannah was in awe of how far the sea stretched.

The hours to fill were many. Each day they had to find a way to take their minds off of the discomforts of stale food and cramped space.

"What shall we play?" asked Louise.

Play, thought Hannah. What a

wonderful word. Here she was, nearly sixteen and learning to play.

"How about school?" she replied.

"School?"

Hannah decided to share her reason.

"I want to learn to read," she said. "And write. You know, I've often wondered if things would have been different for Pa and me if we'd been able to read. Maybe he could have sent a message to me before he died. Maybe I could have seen him …"

Louise gave her such a long, strange look that Hannah thought she'd said something wrong or stupid.

"If you don't want to teach me, it doesn't matter," she mumbled.

"But I do want to!" cried Louise, and once more Hannah was confused by her changing manner.

Chapter 10
Leaving Capetown

After the ship left Capetown, Hannah and Louise were quiet for several days. It was the third port they had visited since leaving England. Hannah had been too seasick to see Tenerife, the first port, while the next one, tropical Rio de Janeiro, had thrilled her.

But Capetown. Capetown had been bleak. When they rowed ashore, Mrs. Marsden had tried to shield the girls from the view of the beach, for it was where the settlement's criminals were flogged or hanged.

Louise went very pale, and days later she was still quiet and barely eating. She appeared to have a pain deep inside that Hannah's friendship could not reach.

Capetown was an important stop. It was the last settlement before Sydney Cove. Many supplies were brought on board, including water in barrels and chickens in cages.

After Capetown, the ship was driven on by the westerlies. These winds were a new discovery, and

Mr. Marsden tried to explain them using a map.

All of Hannah's memories were tied to the other side of the world, and she worried that the great distance she was traveling would weaken them. Sometimes, when she tried to recall the sound of Pa's voice

or the look in his eyes, it was like trying to catch a butterfly in the wind. How much she needed to be sure of her memories, every detail of them! She needed to feel that Pa was with her, beside her, still.

Capetown, with its harsh display of punishments on the beach, had raised other questions, too. *Why* had Pa died? He had been strong and healthy. Had he been flogged like the men she'd seen there? Was he hanged, even?

She wished she had known how to seek out the truth. But, she hadn't known where to start. Meg had only told her about the prison after he'd died.

Hannah felt in the pocket of her

dress and drew out the piece of folded paper she kept hidden there. It was a painting of a river with sunlight striking the water. It was a picture she'd seen in the barbershop window that lonely morning long ago. The sunlight had seemed like a magical pathway, a golden thread that linked her to what she wanted most in the world — Pa.

Did she still feel that link? Or was she cut adrift forever?

Hannah had talked with the boy who'd painted the picture. He had given her food and told her that he had to go away because his mother was ill. He'd talked of his dream to paint.

He would be a young man now. Hannah wished she could have said goodbye to him personally instead of in her heart as she stood near his father's barbershop for the last time.

Her eyes misted over and dropped to find two words written in one corner of the painting. She had learned all her letters now and was beginning to understand words.

"W," she read. W I L L I A M.

She knew that was his name, for she'd heard someone call out to him. The second word began with a T. T U R N E R.

William Turner — I hope you follow your dreams to become a painter, she thought. And as she folded the paper and hid it again, she took a deep breath. Pa was still with her, in her heart. She knew he was.

Once more, the beautiful picture had reassured her.

Chapter 11
Storm

A scream awoke Hannah and she fell from her bunk with a thud. Something heavy crashed into her; then the dark room came alive.

"We've hit a storm!" cried Mr. Marsden.

"Or rocks, more like," said someone.

"Quiet. We need to listen."

Something cracked above them and the whole ship shuddered.

Everyone froze and waited.

"Keep together," said Mr. Marsden. "I'm going up."

A frightened man's voice began rambling. "Van Dieman's Land. That's what we've bumped into. The worst convicts of all are there. And wild animals. If we make it to shore … oh mercy, mercy."

"Shut him up!" cried someone. Then the ship moved as though it had struck a mountain. Hannah felt Louise's hand reaching for hers.

"I've gotten wet!" cried Louise.

"Like the whales," said Hannah. "Just pretend we're whales. They all kept together in the waves, remember?"

Mr. Marsden lurched back to them.

"They've battened down. I couldn't see. The sailors are handling it."

"We're trapped. Doomed," the frightened man droned on.

"Keep it down."

"Watch out!"

Panic took over, heightened by each pitch of the ship. Then came a grinding crunch and the scream, "We're breaking up!"

Everyone fell quiet. There was only one focus — listening. As they waited for the next loud sound, each small one took on meaning. Dripping, splashing, knocking, rocking, all against the background roar of the waves.

Then a new sound threaded its way through the darkness. It was Mrs. Marsden, singing. The words of the hymn wouldn't come, but she forced the tune from her throat.

Slowly the others picked it up, and those not singing were calmed.

Minutes passed.

The minutes became hours.

Just before the gray dawn, the night was at its darkest.

The passengers had grown tired and arguments erupted.

Louise wished her family could be apart from the others. She felt sure they would all die. She wanted John with them, yet she was glad he would be spared. When would it happen? The *waiting* was unbearable. Would the wind hurl them into a cliff or would they simply sink, down, down, down to the sea's depths?

What if they were separated? What if *some* of them lived?

What if Hannah alone survived and never *knew*?

"Mama, Papa, she has to know," she cried.

"You tell her, dear," said Papa, and she knew then that he, too, thought they might die.

"Hansy," she sobbed, and Hannah's heart froze. The moment had come for Louise's secret. They weren't going to keep her with them after all. They'd just used her like Mrs. Carver had in order to get help with the children. To amuse them. Once they reached the colony, she would be on her own. Again.

She sat motionless in the dark.

"Hannah," said Louise, trying again. "Your father ... no ... you know how my father said your cottage might be sold later, maybe, after the papers are signed?"

"I don't want to know," said Hannah flatly, but Louise continued.

"Father went to the magistrate in Bow Street and to the prison, and he found out your father was …"

Hannah's cold, aching body tensed. He was what? Flogged? Hanged?

"Don't say it! Don't say it!" she screamed and pushed Louise aside.

Toby yelled. Louise struggled back.

"Listen to me, Hansy," she cried. "We were waiting till we were sure. He might be alive. In the colony. Meg lied when she said he was dead. They sent him to the colony as a convict, years ago."

Chapter 12
The Man in the Field

A bronzed man stood in a field.

The spade that he held was useless.

The soil was hard enough in this part of the world without having useless tools, too.

It was not the work that irked him, but the time that it took. For Tom Brand, too much time had passed already. Way too much. Even now that he was a freed man, with his leave papers and a land grant, only one thing really mattered to him — buying a passage home so he could go and look for his daughter, Hannah.

In many ways, he wanted to stay. To make this his home. His skills lay in growing food from the soil, and he was gradually learning the secrets of the soil near Sydney Cove. But somewhere across the world was his little girl. He had tried to send news to her whenever he could — from the prison and from the ports — but never, since the day of his arrest, had he heard word of her.

Tom Brand's eyes moved to his timber shack where chickens scratched and one scraggly bush of rosemary grew. The memory of another house in another land washed over the scene.

Drat this spade, he thought bitterly. Now he'd have to buy a new one, and that would take both precious time and money.

Chapter 13
Sydney Cove

The morning was fine with a golden sun and a gentle breeze. It was perfect for bringing in a tall ship that had one mast gone and a beam that had been damaged on some rocks.

A noisy crowd had gathered on the shore to watch the ship draw near. In the crowd stood a silent, bronzed man who needed to buy a spade. His boots covered scars left by irons around his ankles — reminders of his convict years, reminders that would stay with him always. He was thin from past illnesses, but a fiery determination made him strong.

The man watched the people now crowding onto the deck. No soldiers or chains were in sight. One day, he dreamed, he too would travel as a free man …

Suddenly, he froze. He had seen her — a tall girl with a cloud of golden hair. Roughly he rubbed his eyes with his fists, fighting the mist that formed in them, trying to blot out the cruel vision. For it couldn't be her. He knew that.

He looked again at the ship, and the vision remained. The girl was stretching forward as though searching along the shore. Beside her, holding her arm, a second girl stood.

The man no longer heard the raucous clatter and chatter around him, for through the air came one long, piercing cry.

"Pa!"

"Hannah," he breathed, then went racing forward, shouting her name to the sky.